Can You Get Our Ball?

Story by Linda Strachan
Pictures by David Mostyn

We went to play football.

The ball went up in a tree.

3

Mum looked up.

Mum went to get our ball.

9

We played football again.

"Can you get our ball?"

"I can't get the ball," said Mum.

Dad looked up.

The ball was on the roof.

Dad went to get a ladder.

He went up on the roof.

We all looked up.
"Can you get our ball?"

"No," said Dad. "I can't get it."